Look at the Flowers

:Coloring Book 1

by
Snow Marie Reese

Look at the Flowers
:Coloring Book 1
by Snow Marie Reese
Copyright © 2015 Twin Scale Media LLC

First Printing, 2015
ISBN: 978-1517307851
Twin Scale Media LLC
Colorado Springs, Co

www.twinscalemedia.com

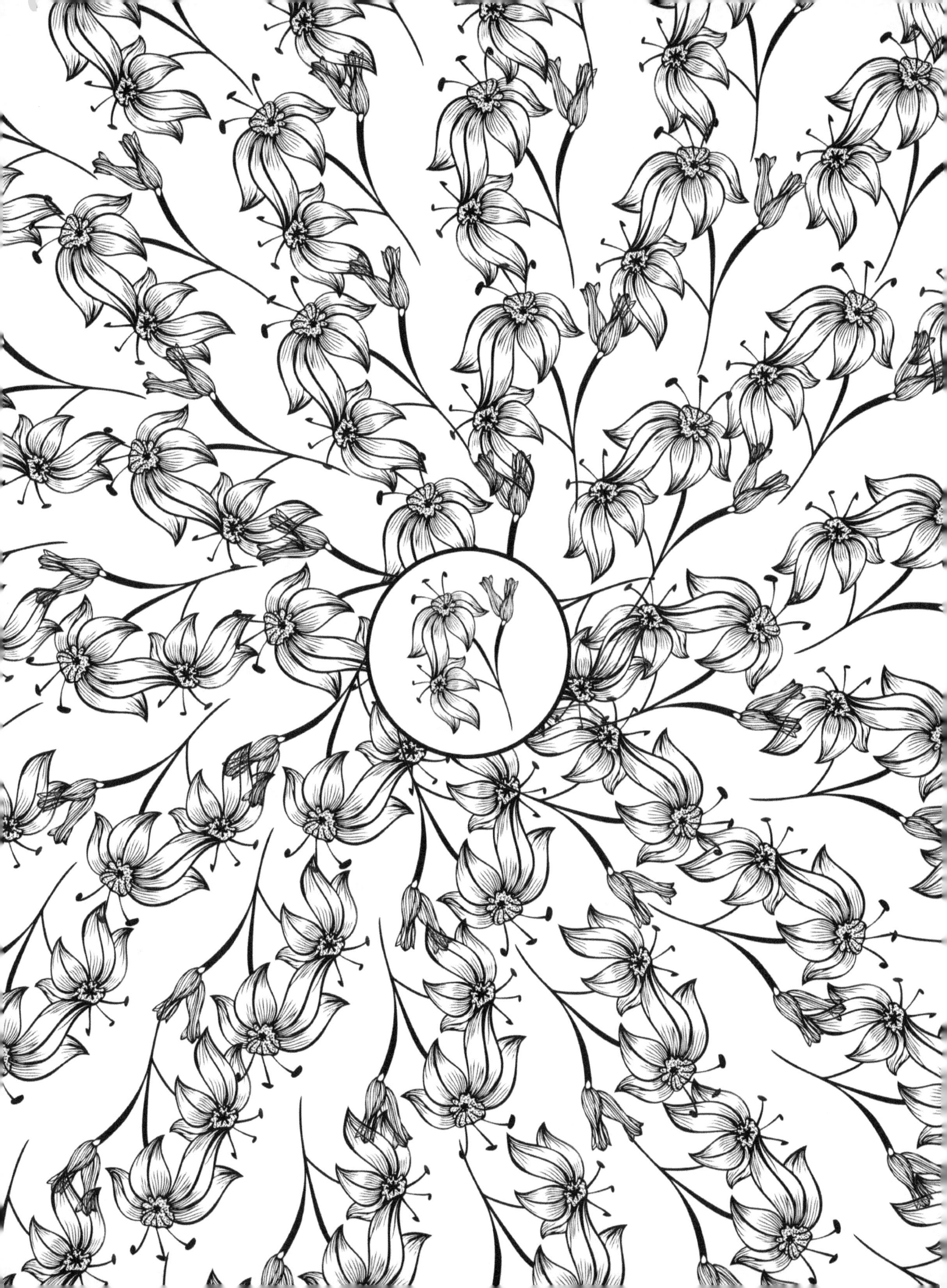

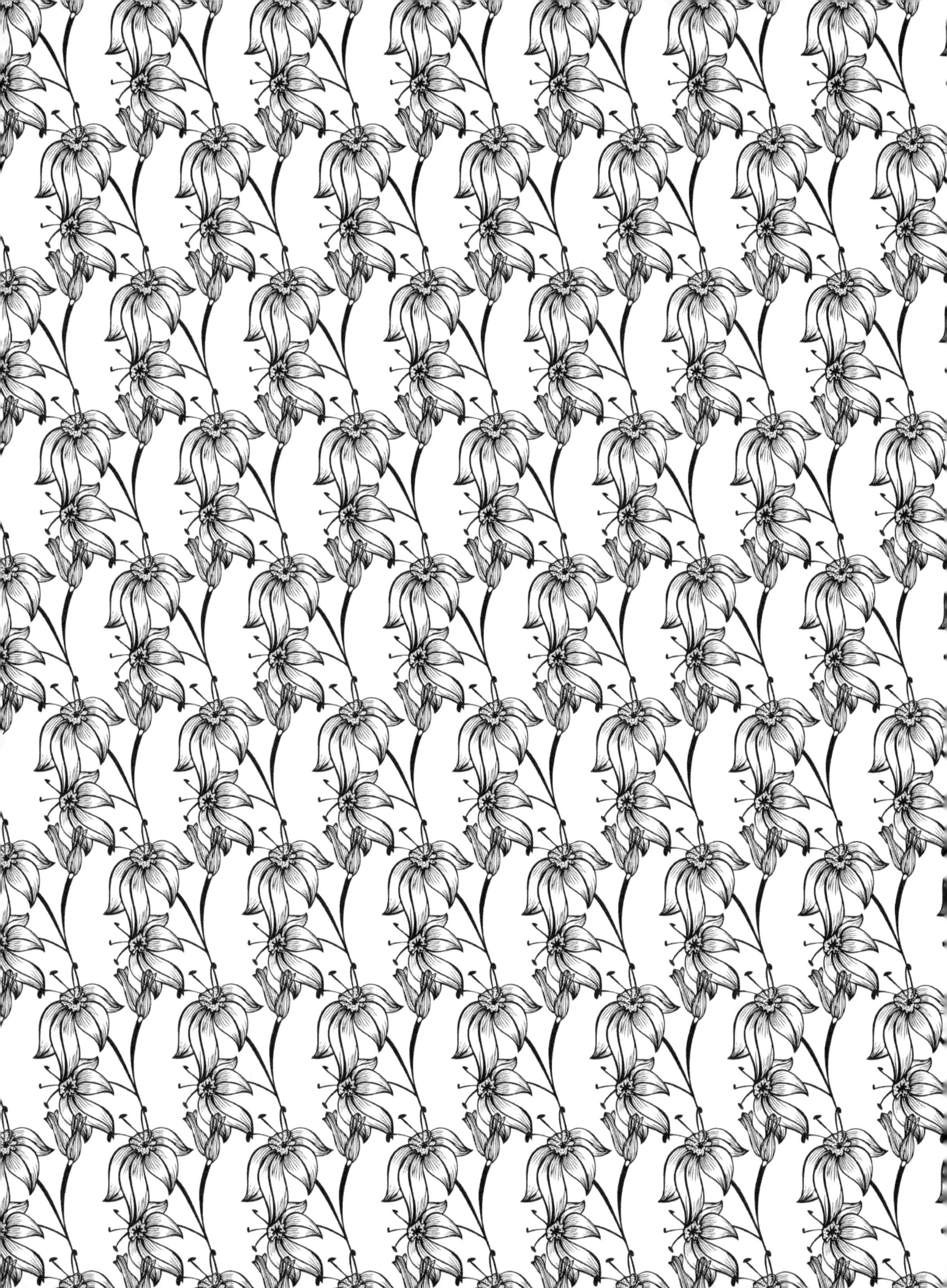

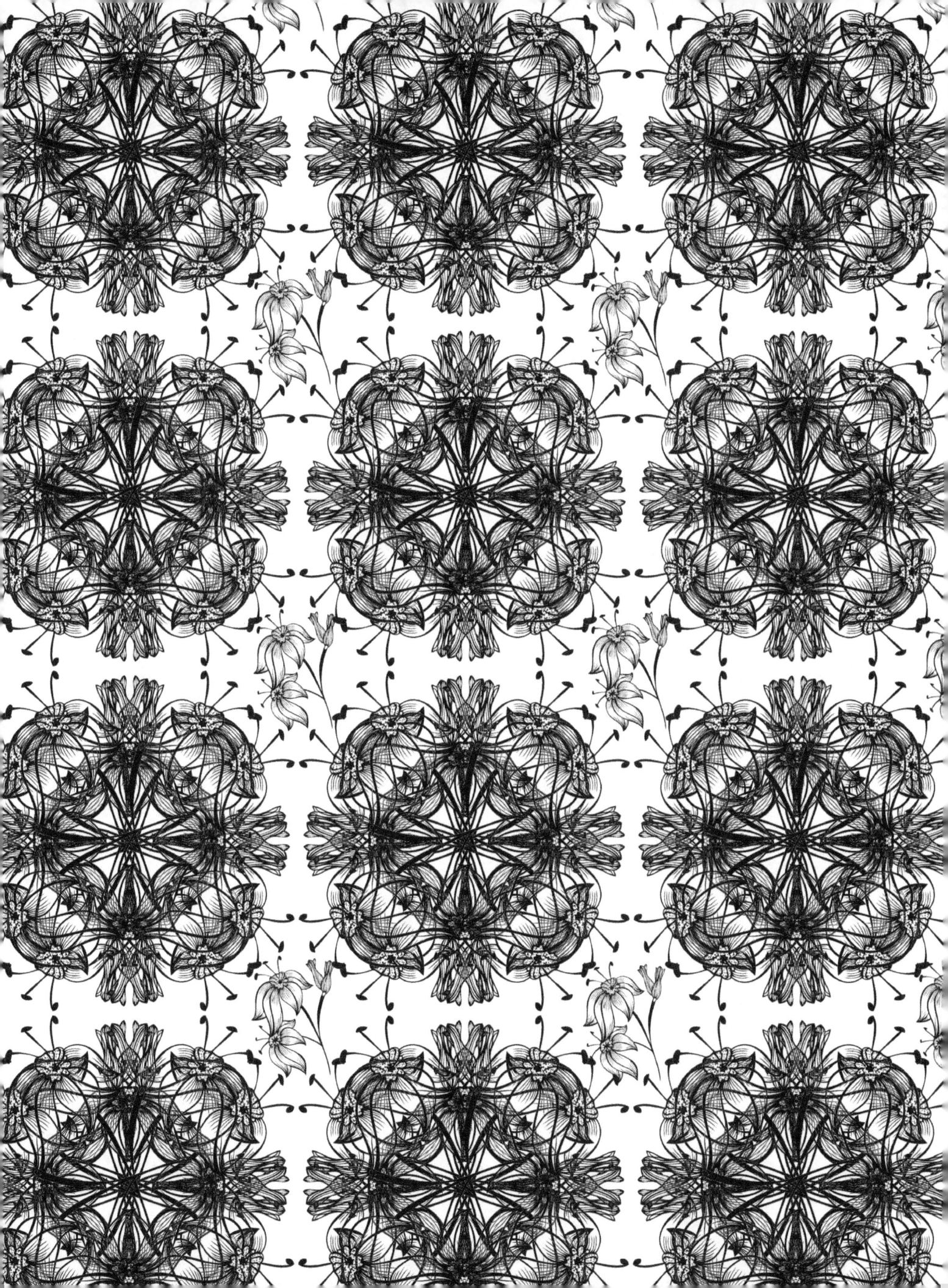

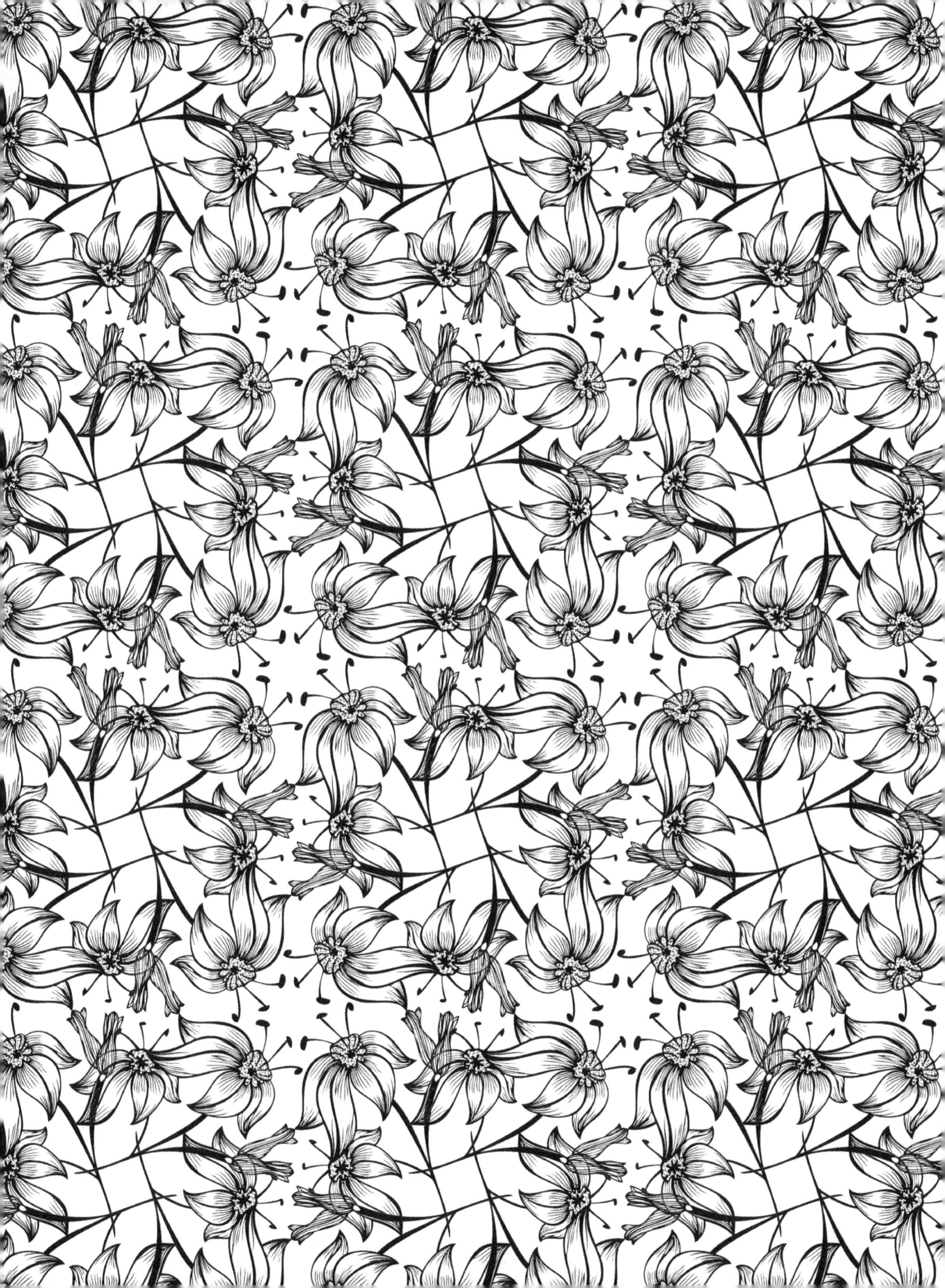

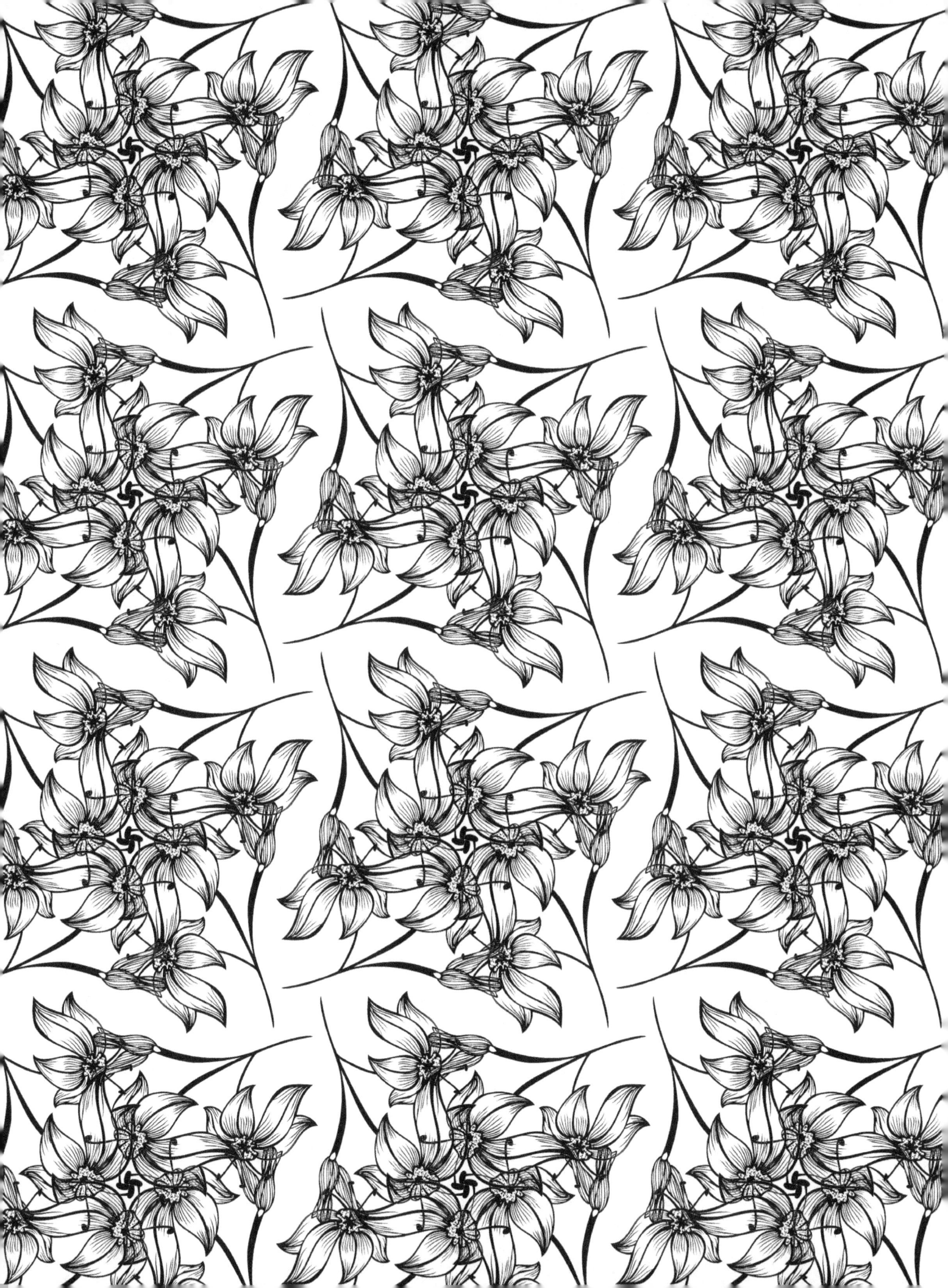

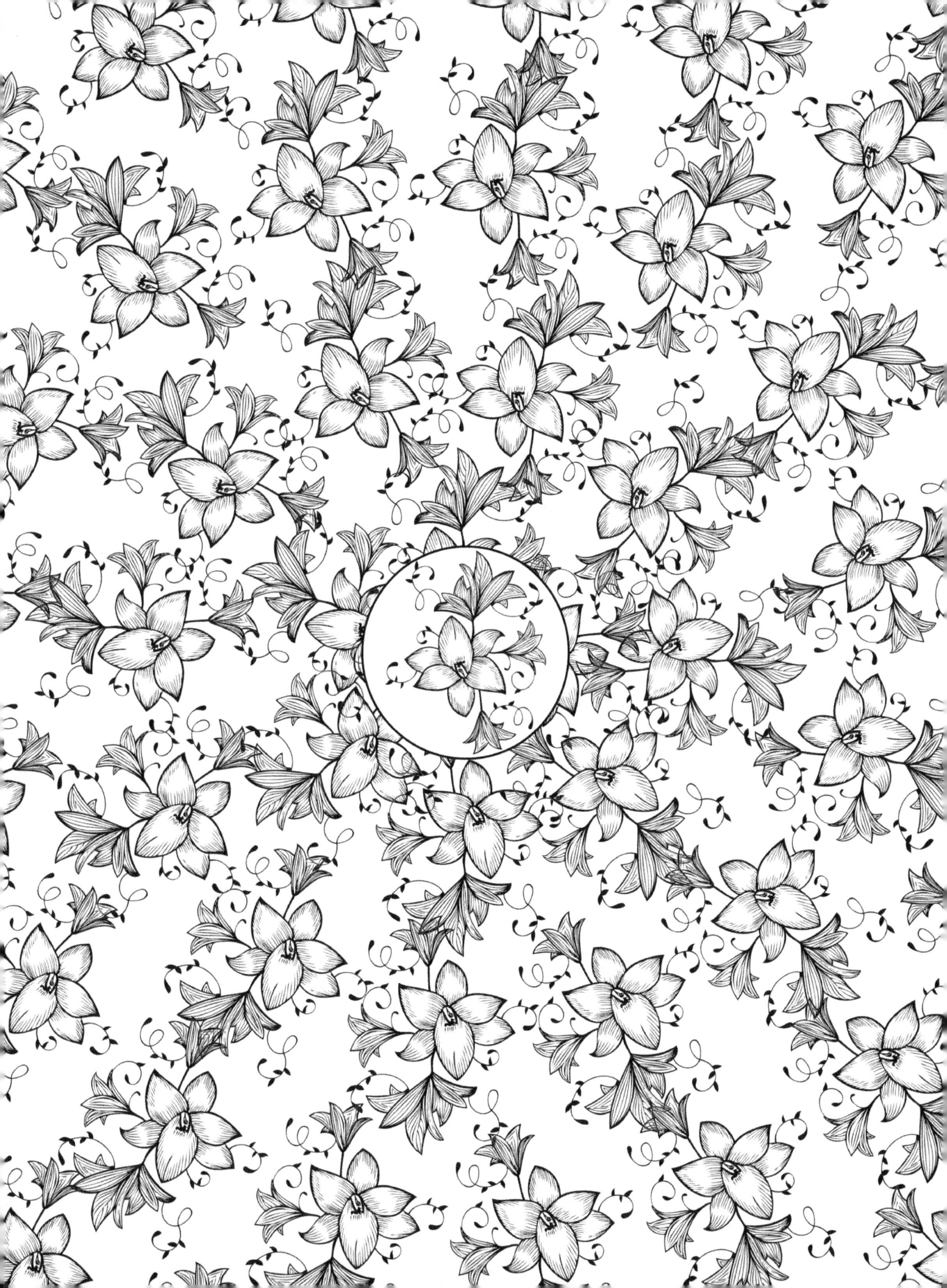

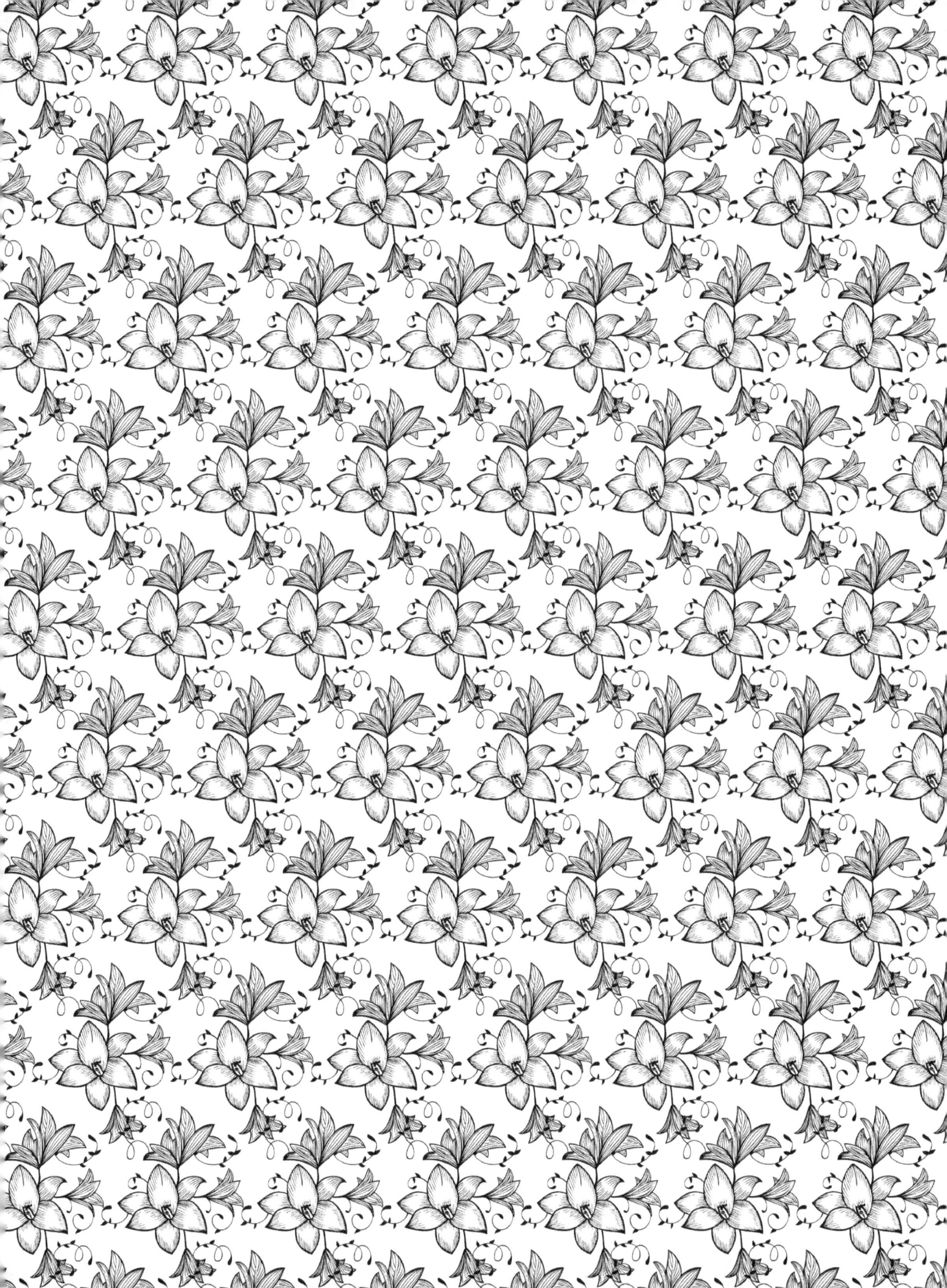

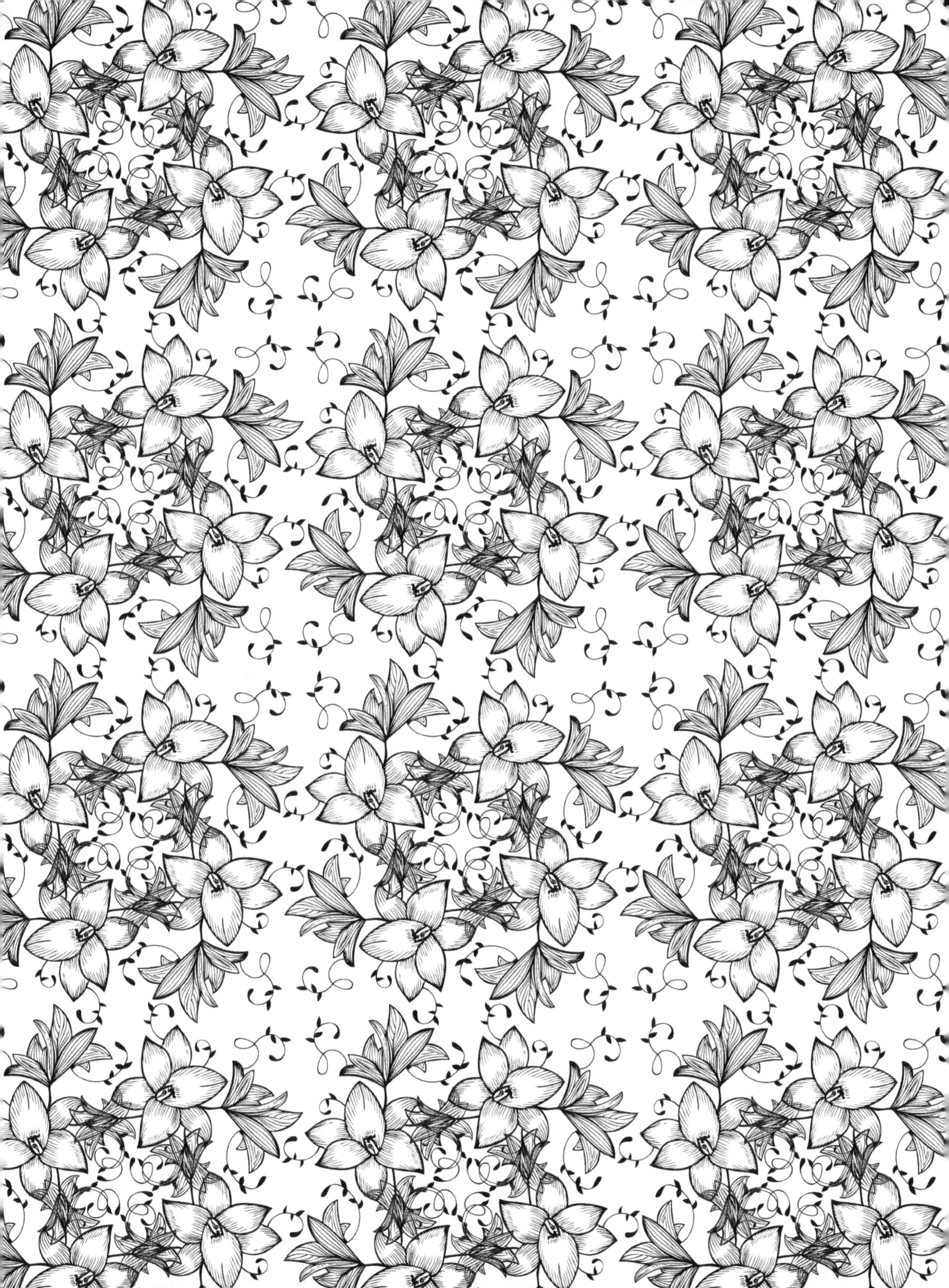

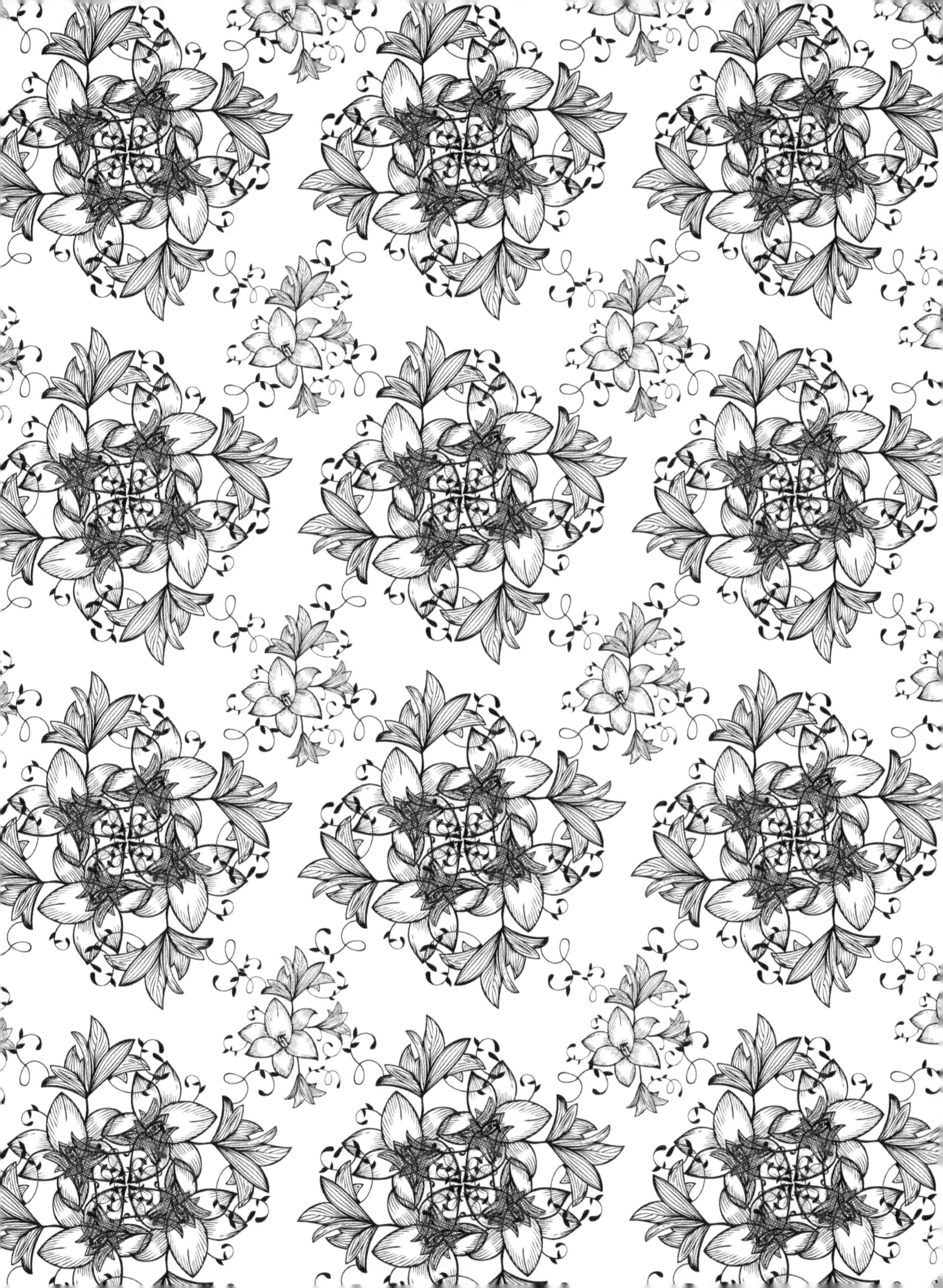

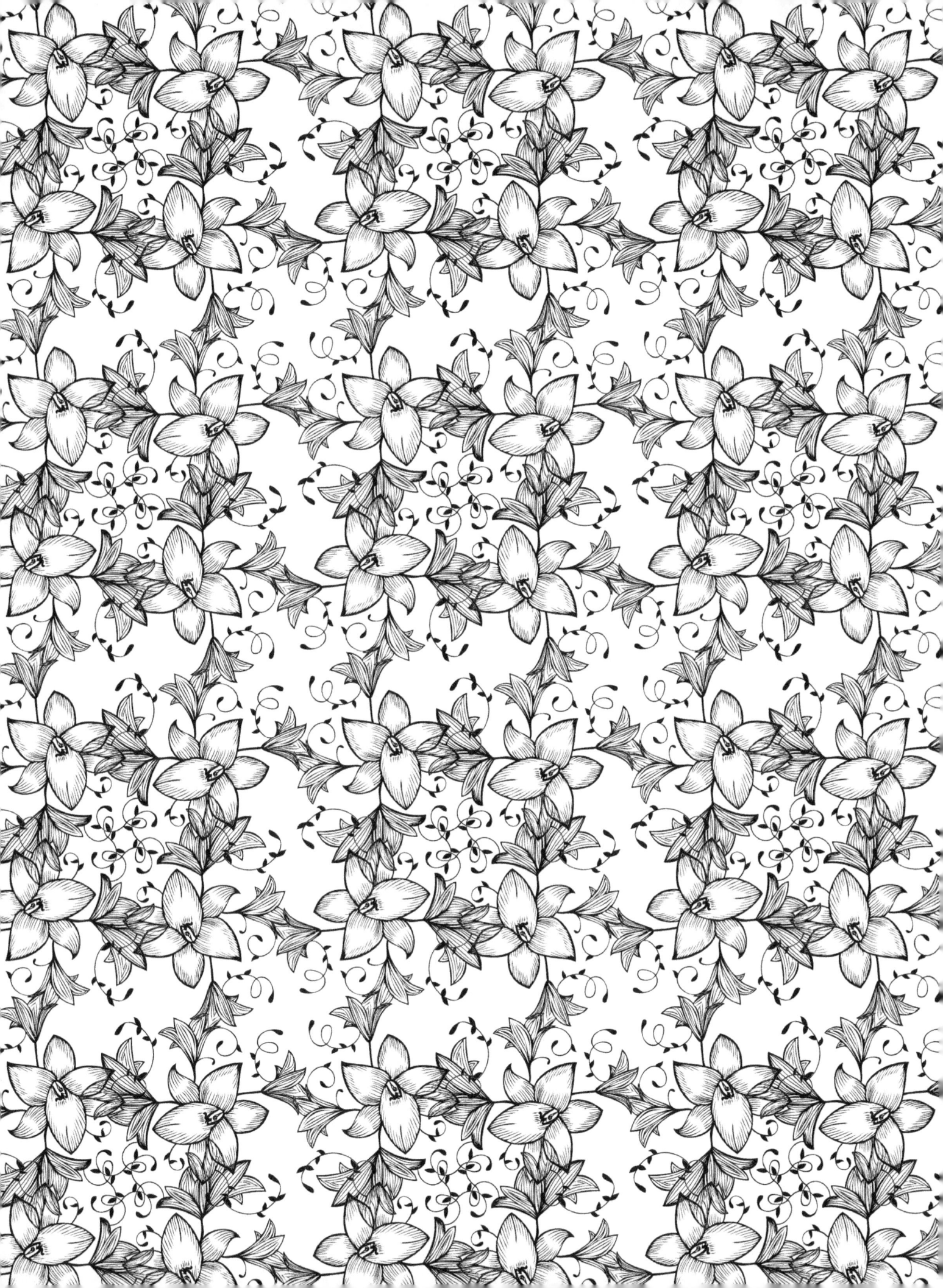

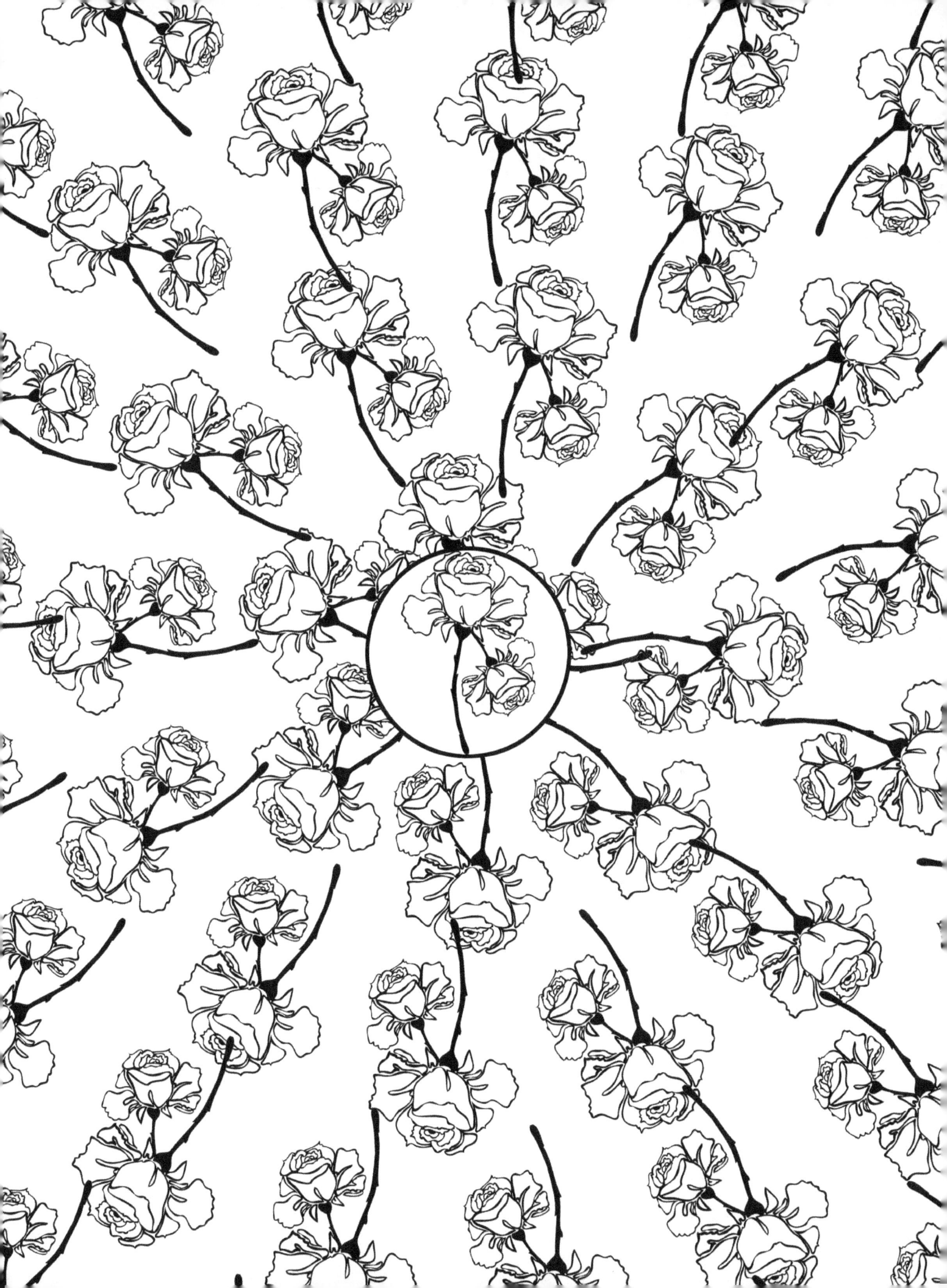

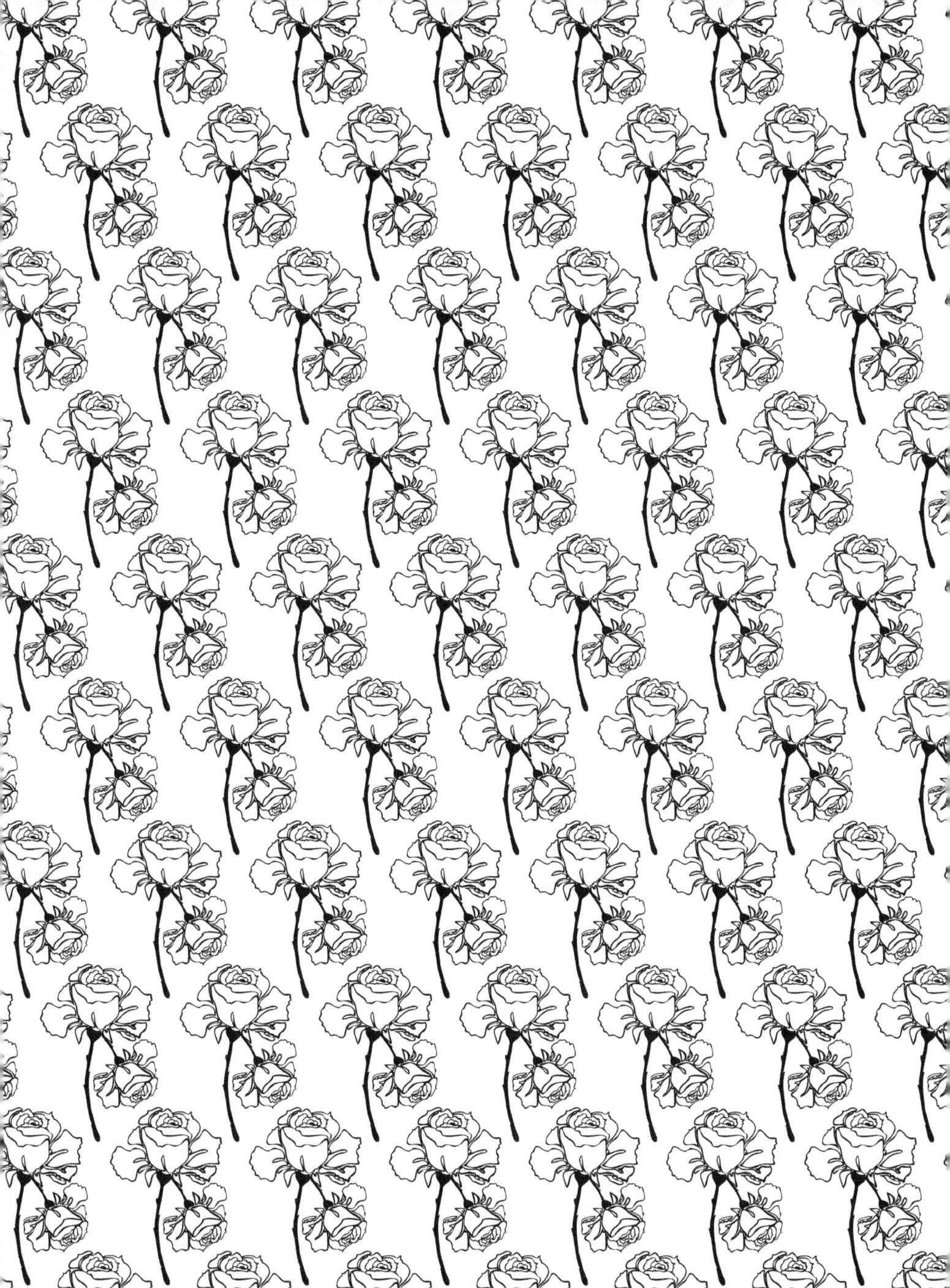

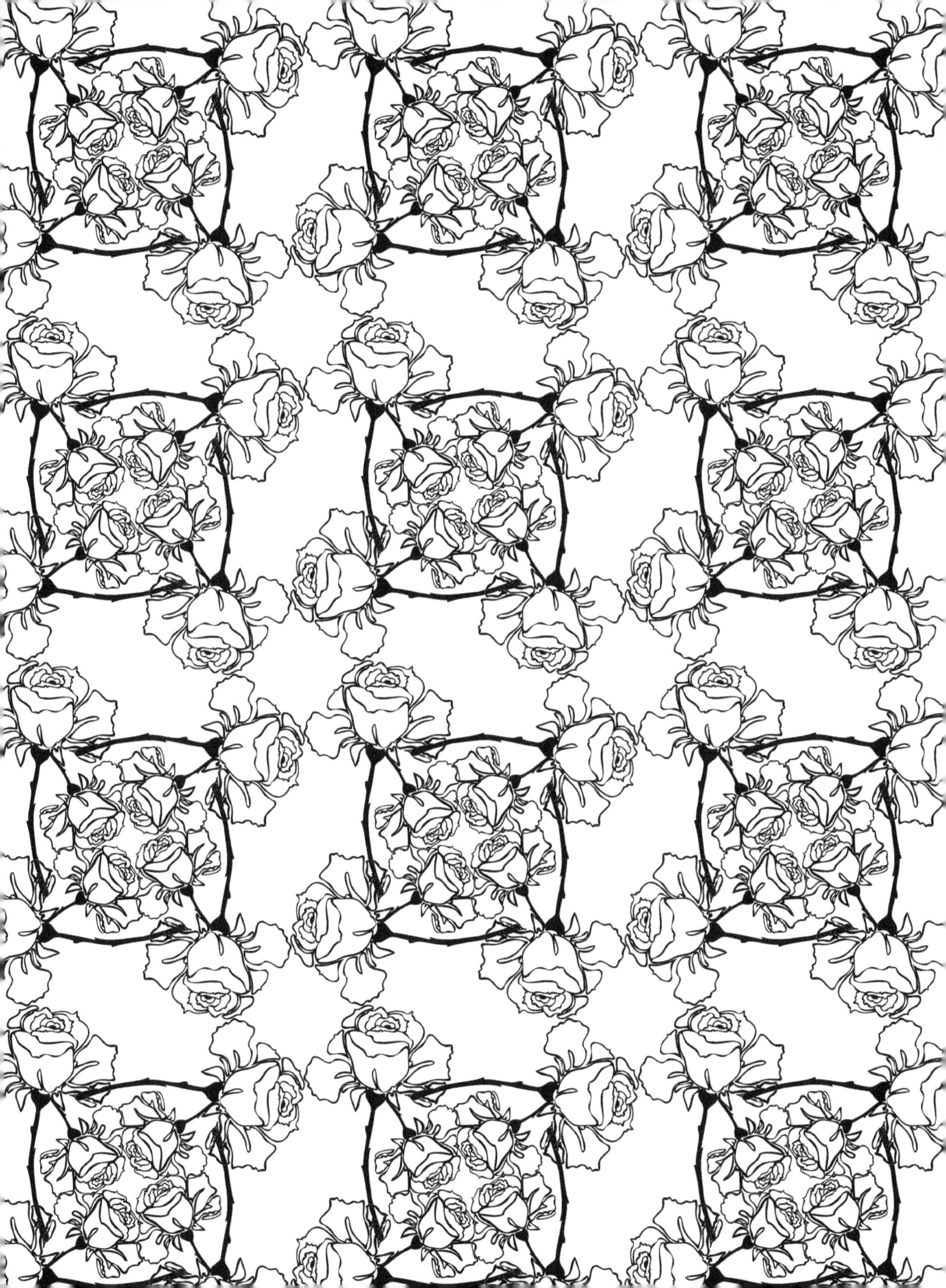

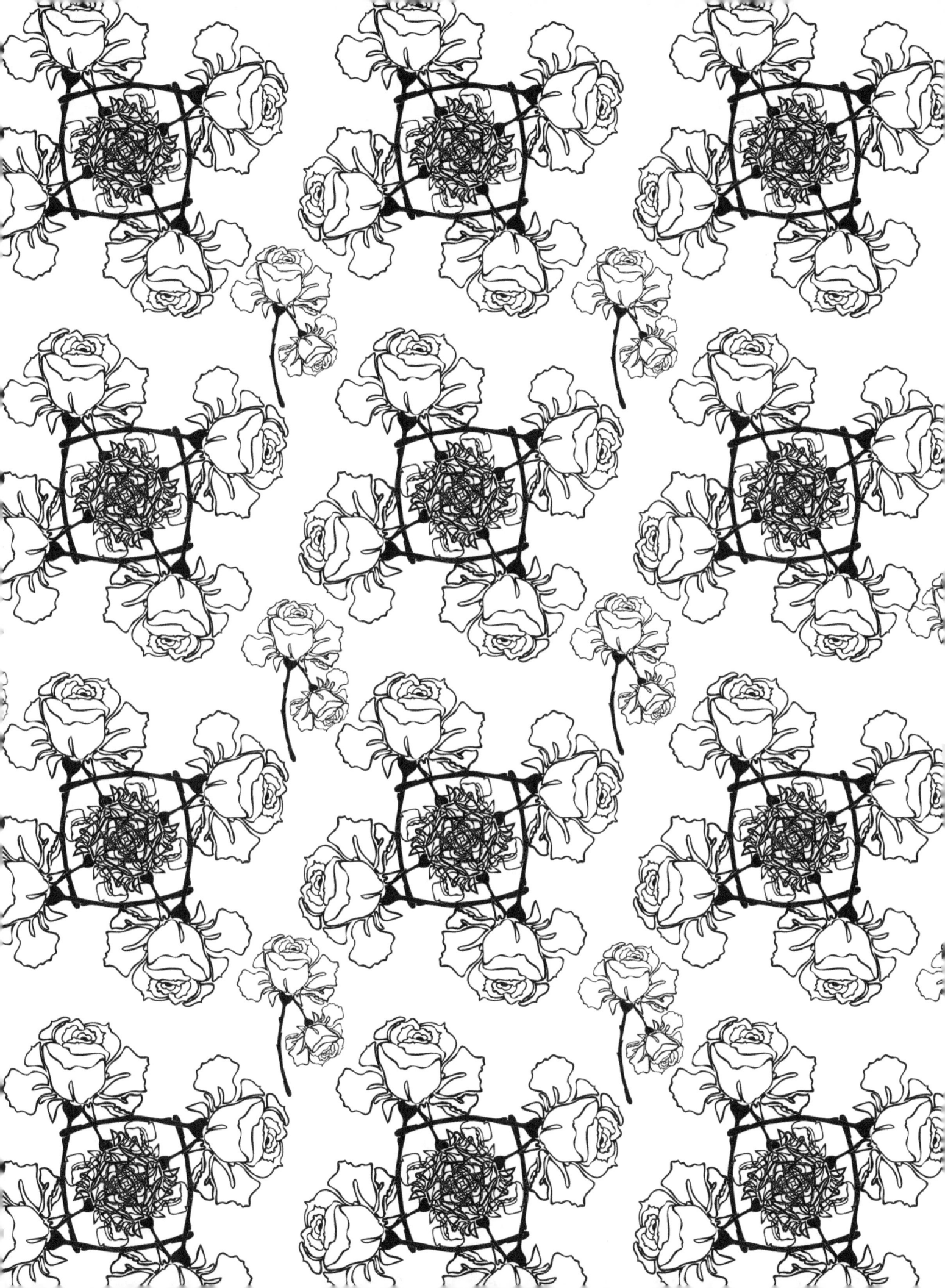

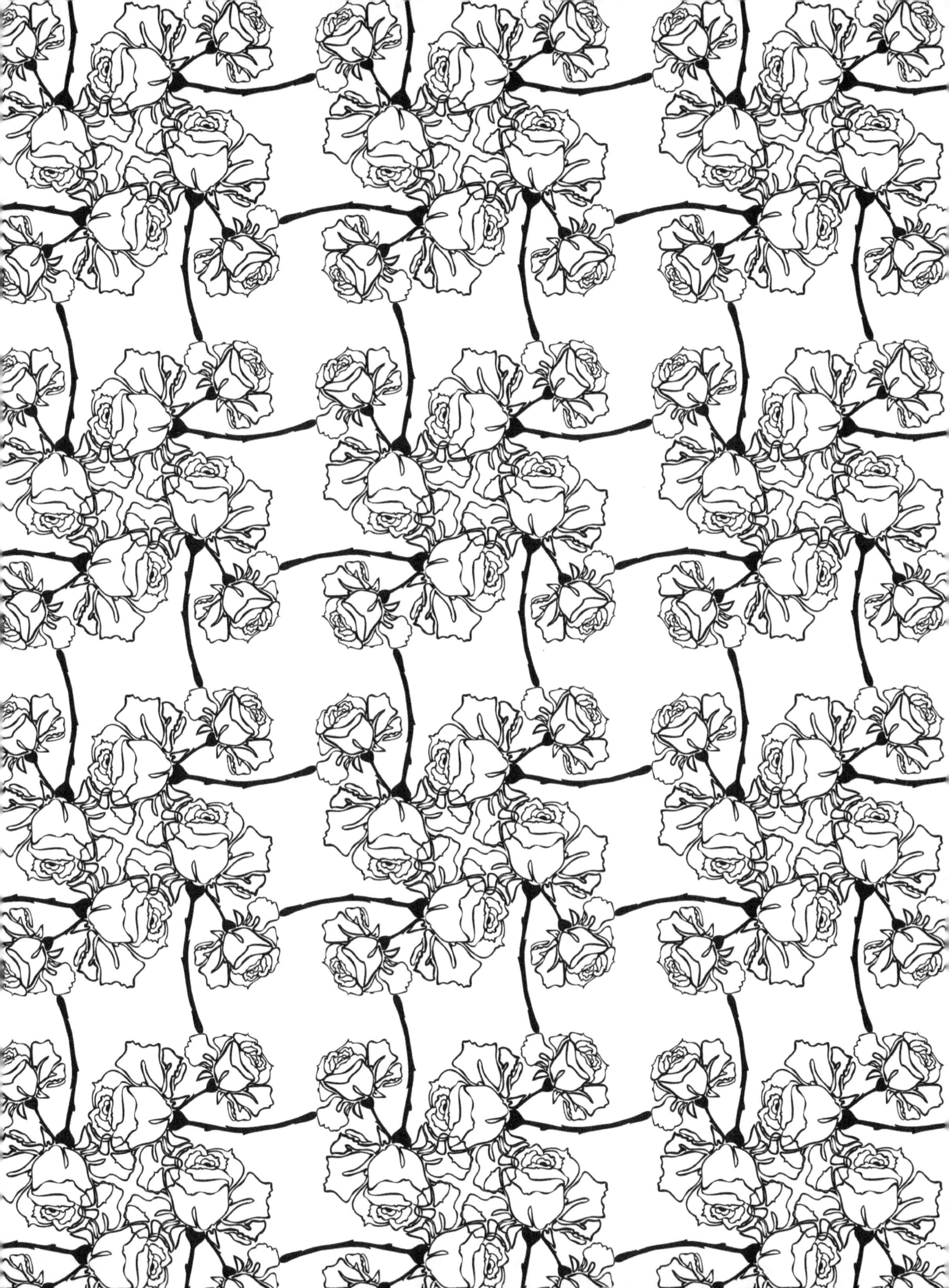

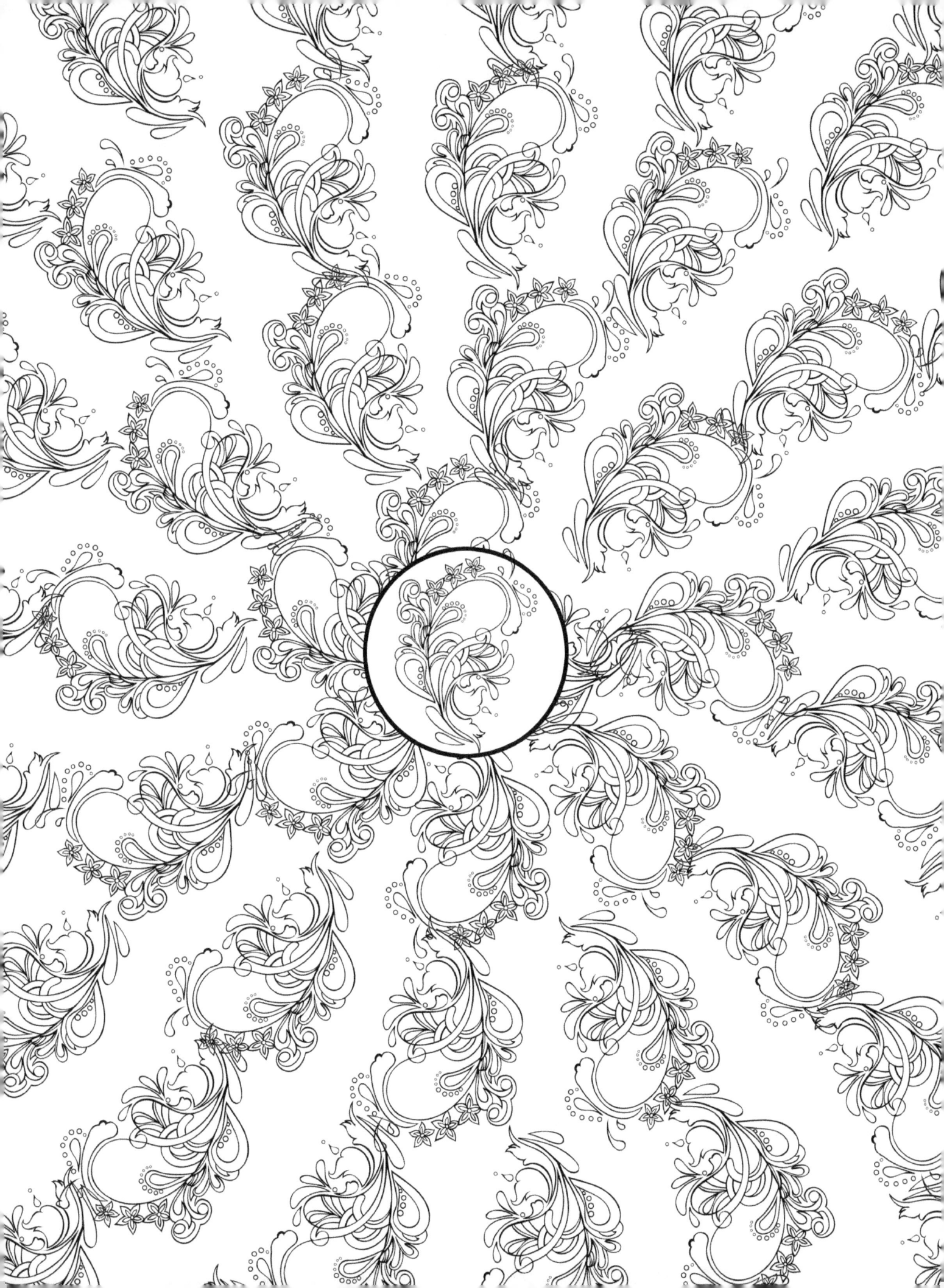

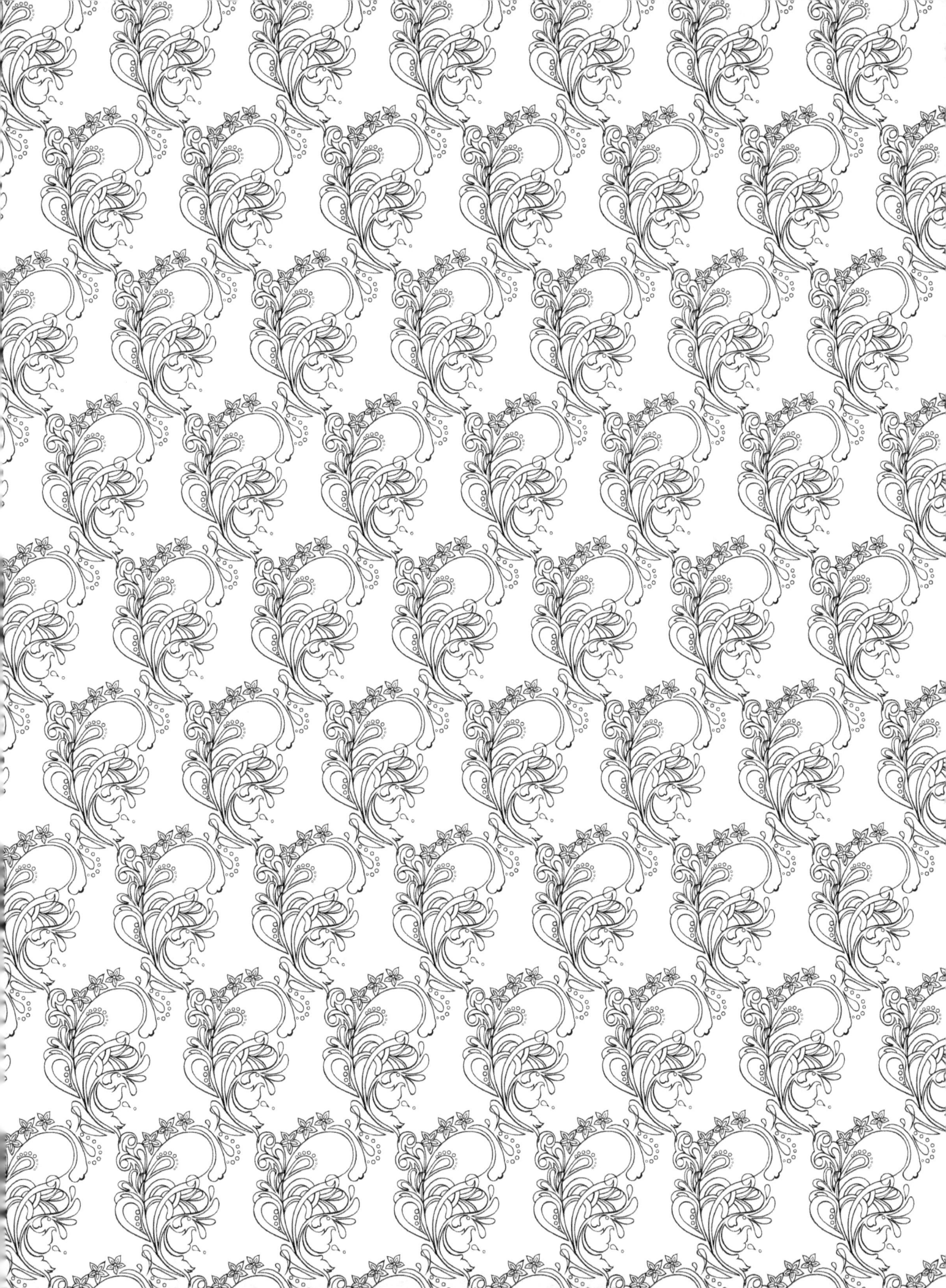

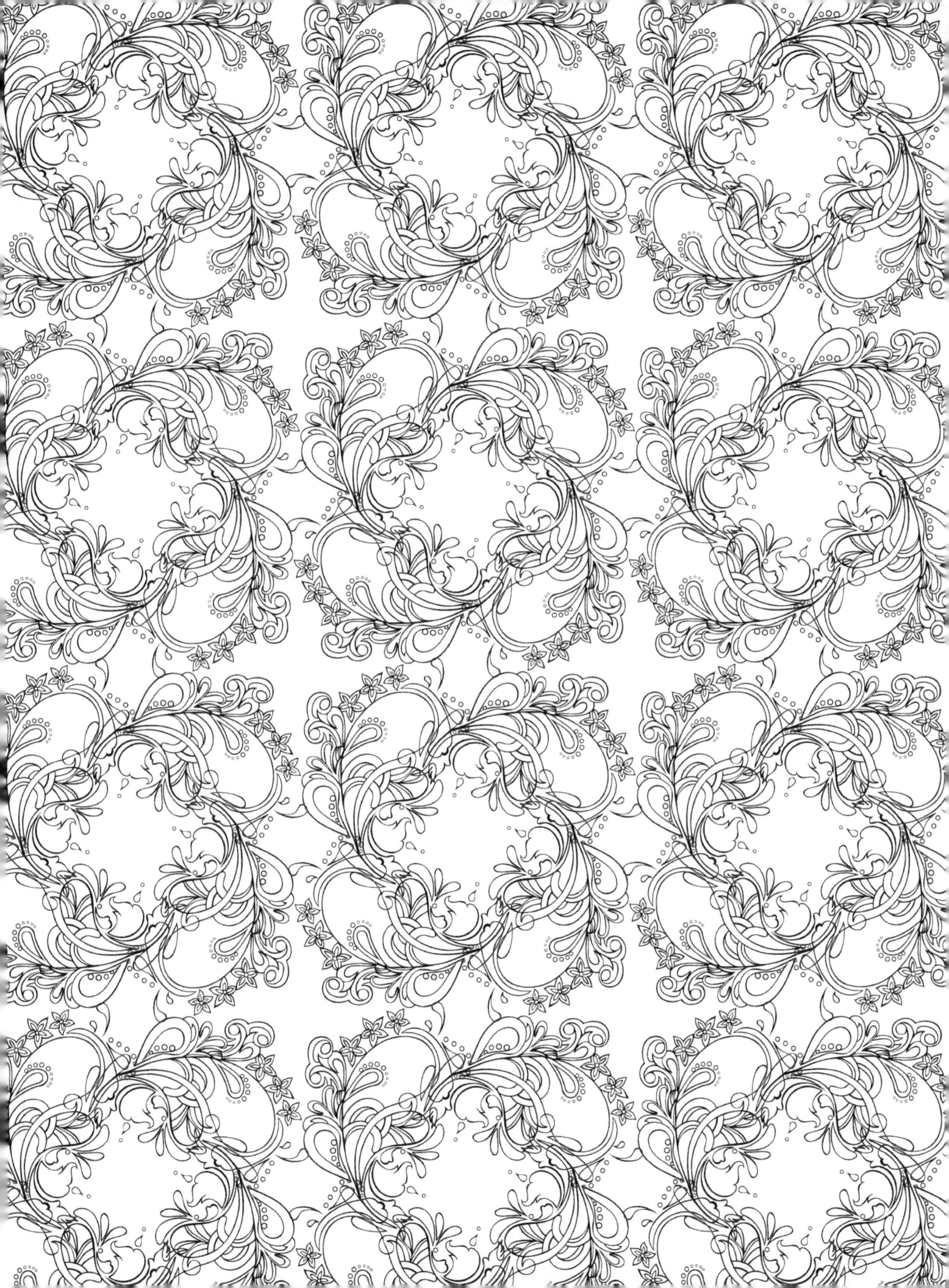

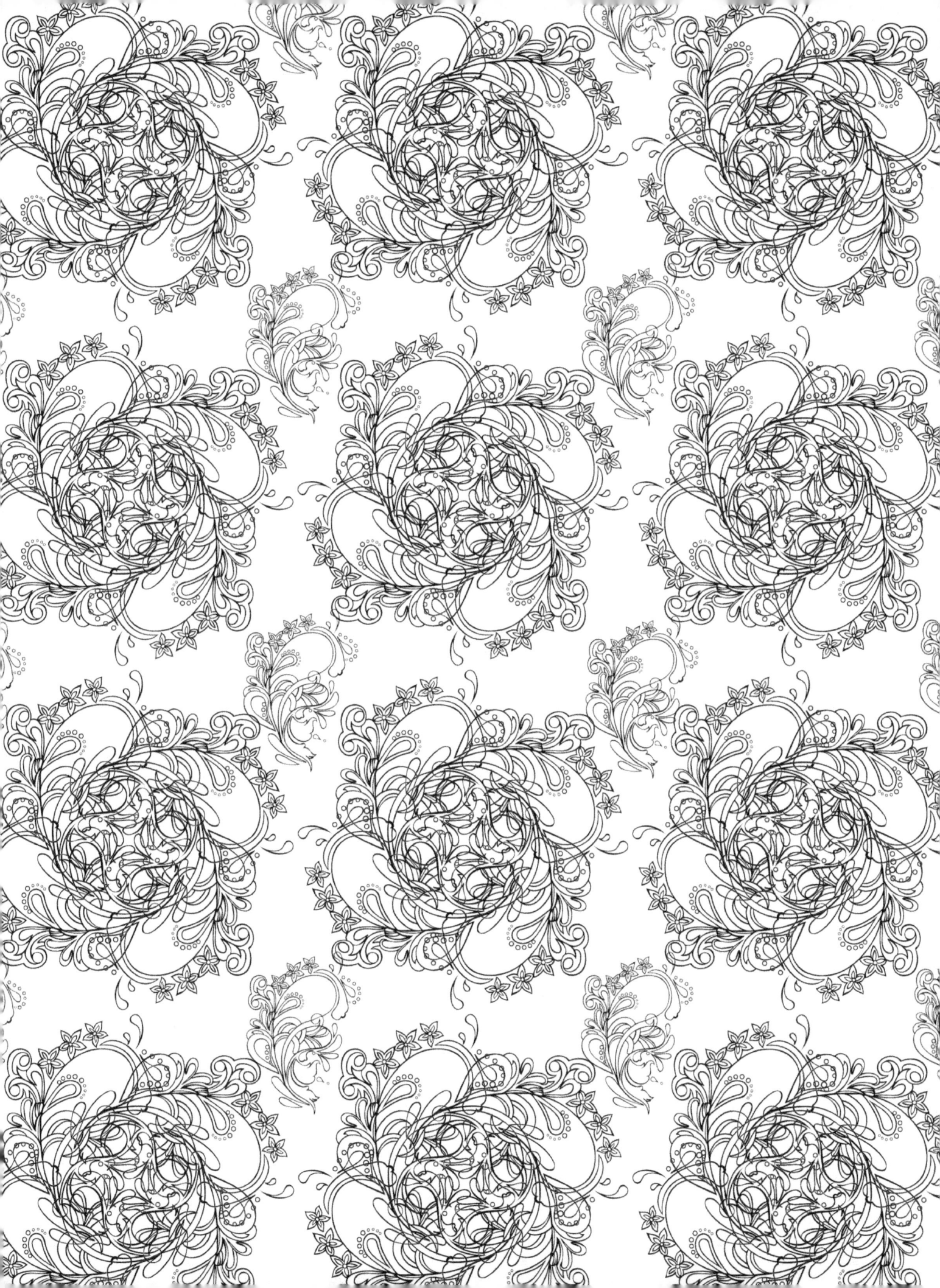

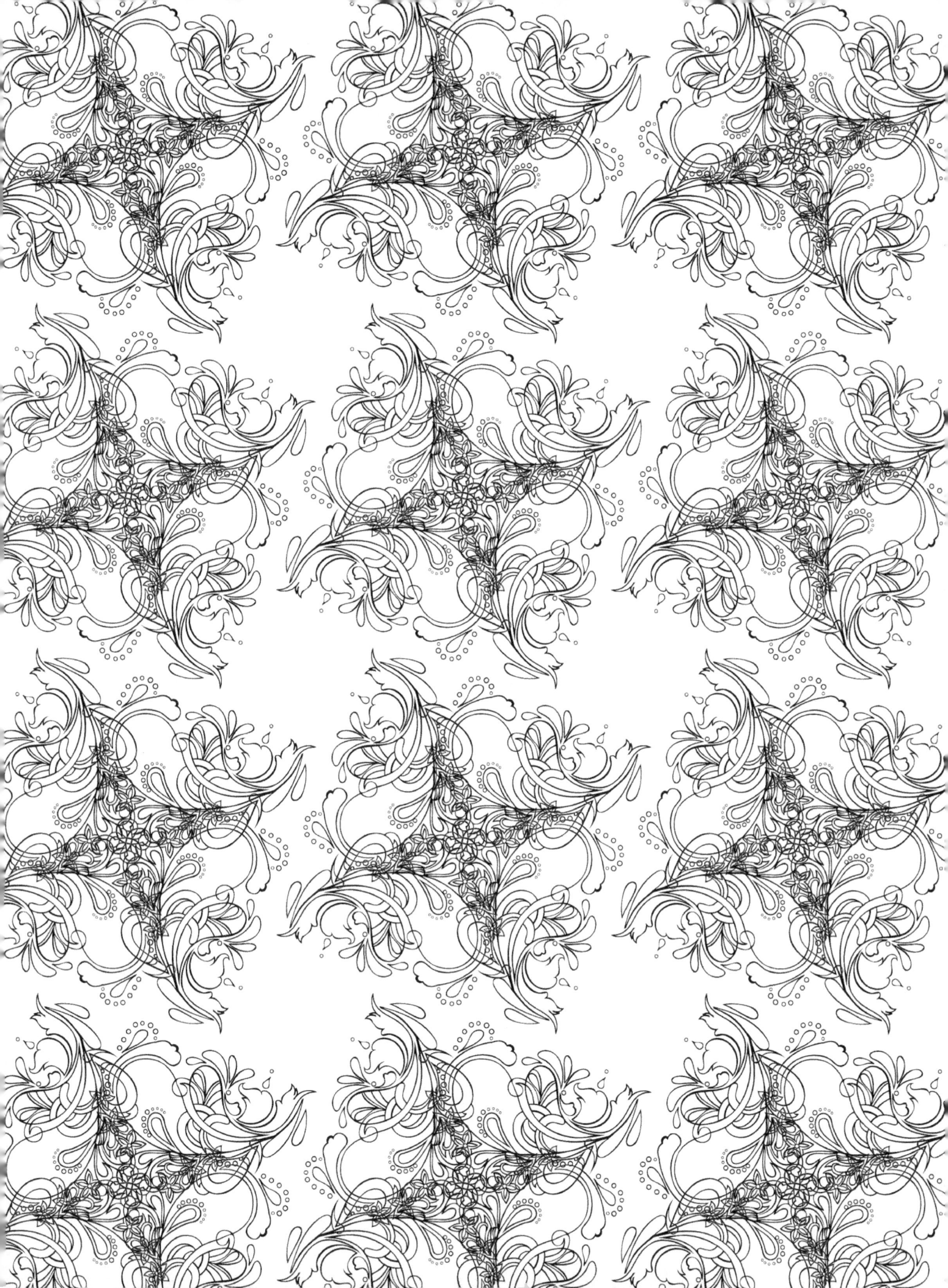

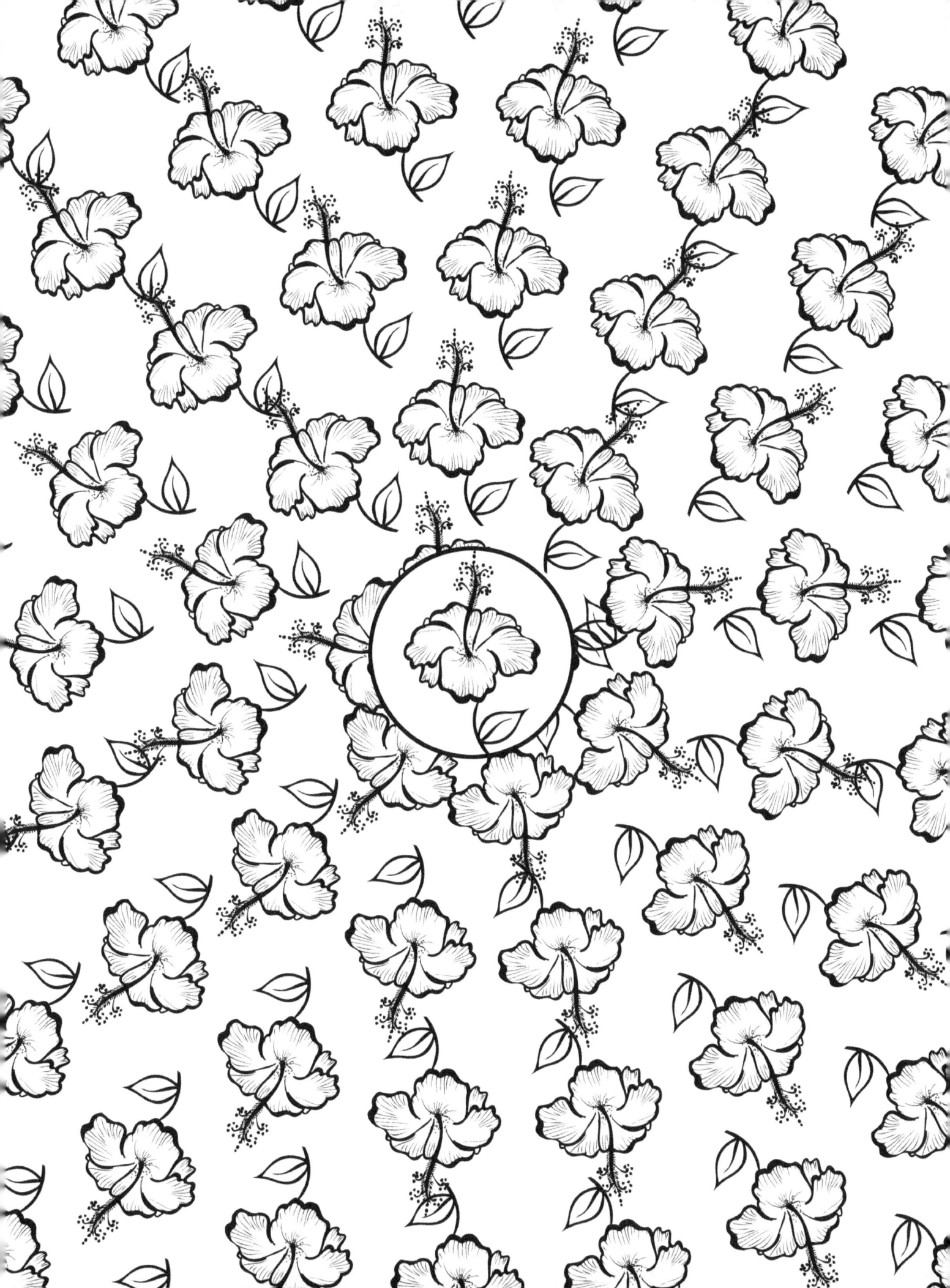

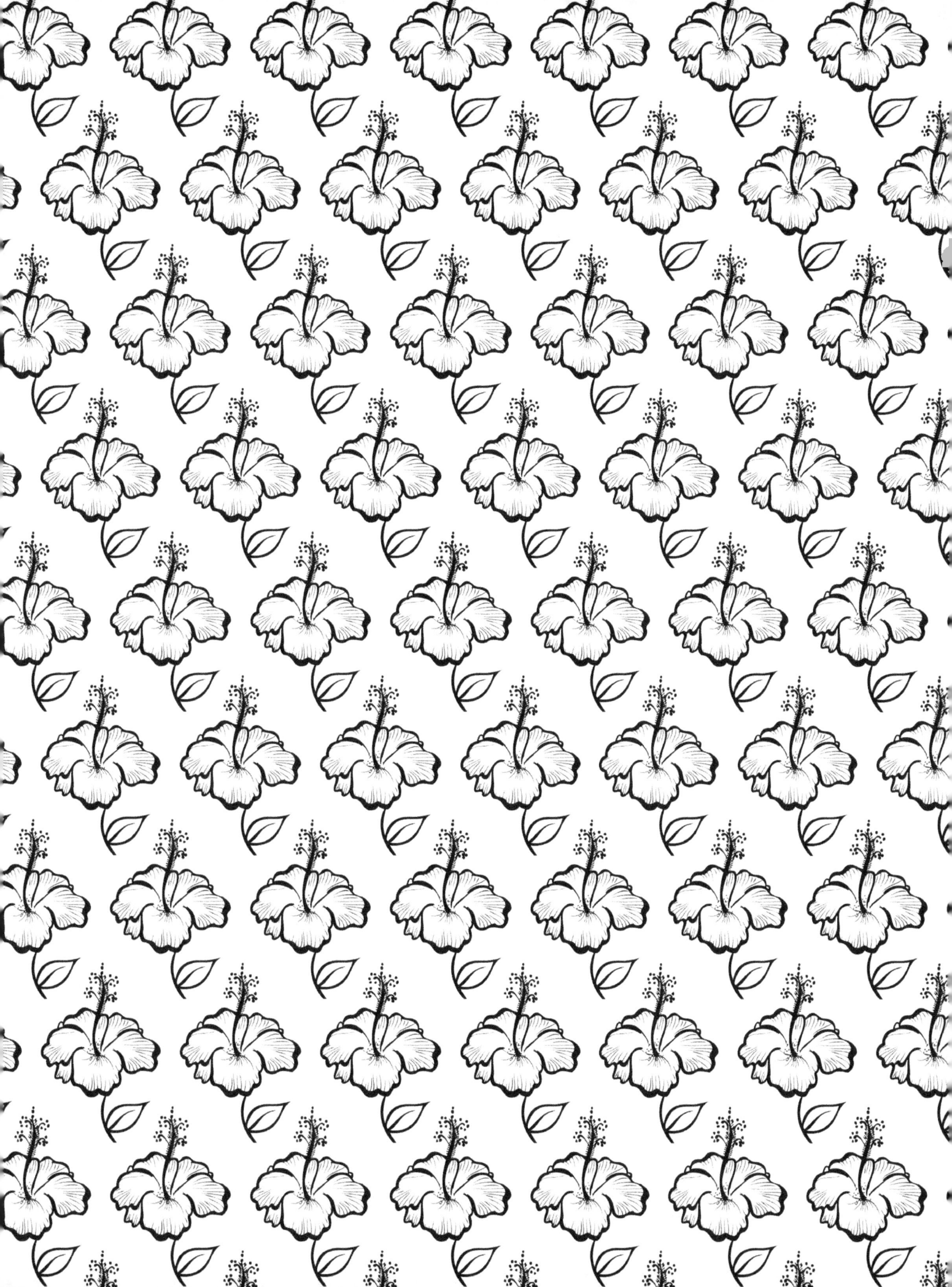

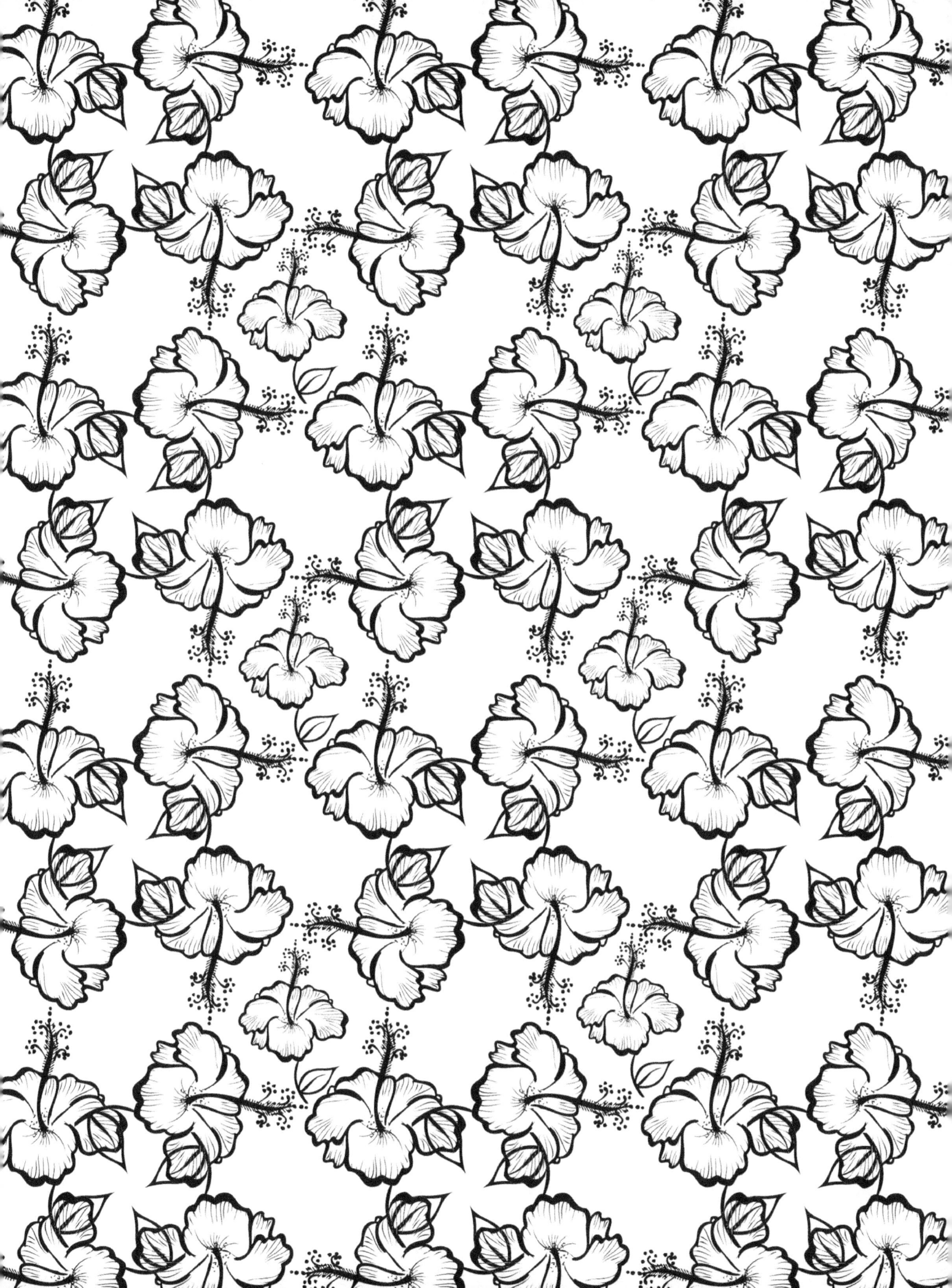

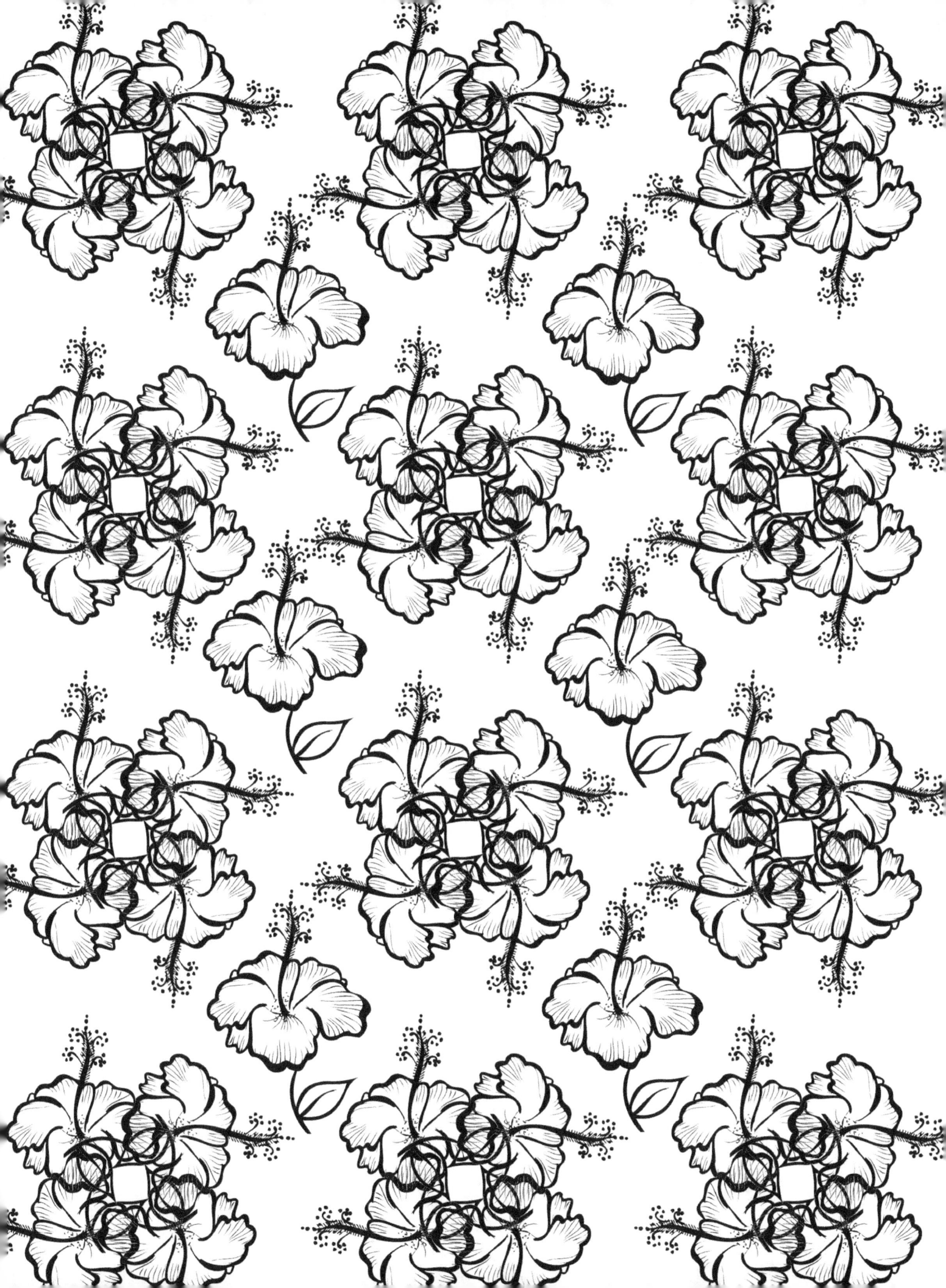

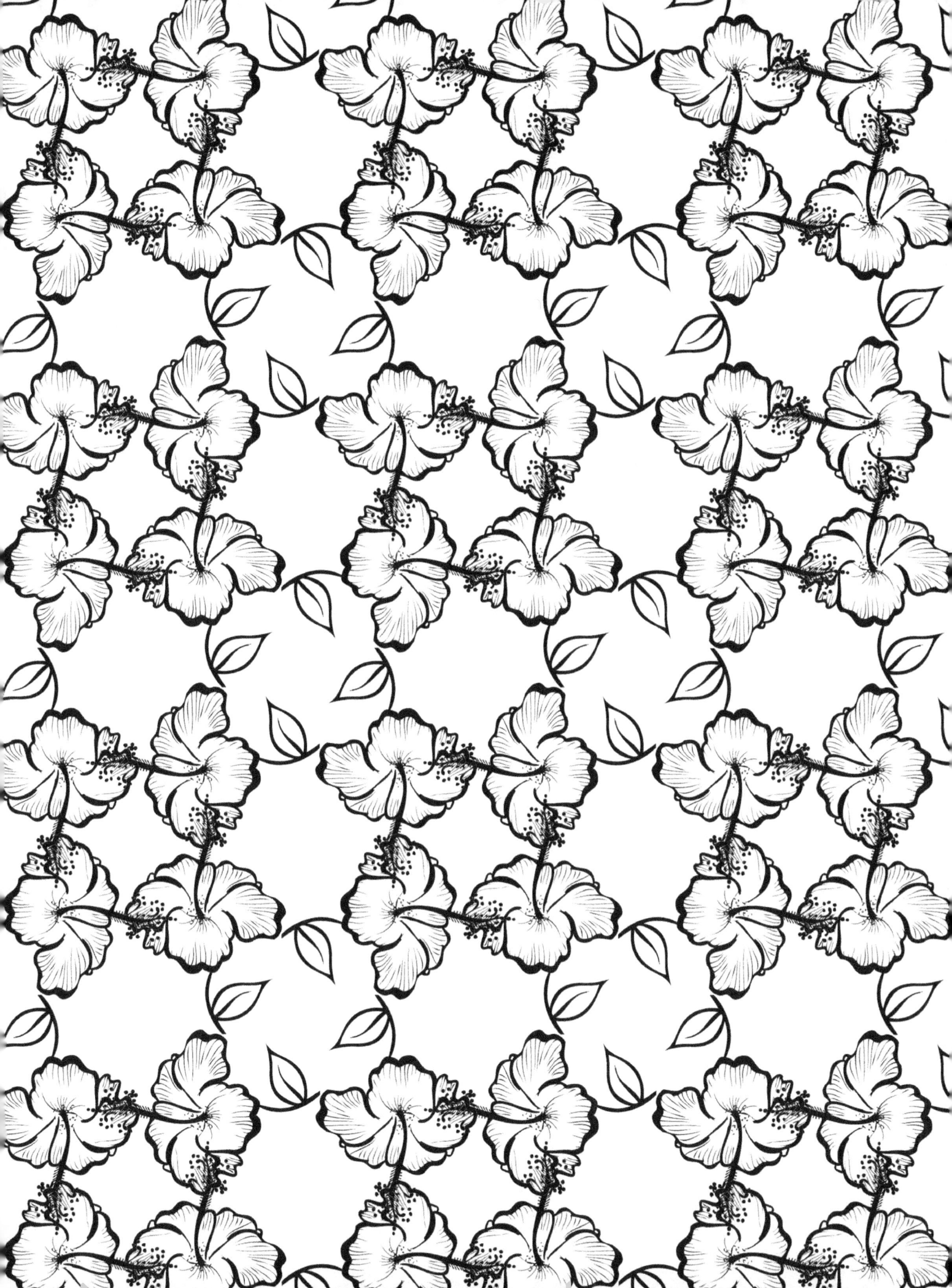

ABOUT THE AUTHOR

Snow Marie Reese is a photographer and filmmaker currently living in Colorado Springs. She has a Bachelor of Arts in Film and Video Production specalizing in visual effects. She enjoys cosplay and spending most of her days working on films.